I, AI

Preparing for Tomorrow's Jobs in the Musk Era

Christian A. Dickinson

Learning Engineered Publishing

All rights reserved. International copyright secured.

Title: *I, AI*
Subtitle: *Preparing for Tomorrow's Jobs in the Musk Era*
Written by: Christian A. Dickinson

Illustrations by: Learning Engineered LLC
Published by: Learning Engineered Publishing®

Library of Congress Control Number:
ISBN (Print): 978-1-965741-62-7

Second Edition: 2026

Printed & Created in: United States of America

Learning Engineered Publishing® (U.S. Reg. No. 8,057,038) is a division of Learning Engineered, LLC, and a subsidiary of Carpe Diem Unlimited Holdings, Inc.

LEARNING ENGINEERED
PUBLISHING

Contents

DEDICATION

For my three new autodidactic friends. You chose to take learning into your own hands, and in doing so, helped me see more clearly the world ahead of us. This book is written in preparation for a world that does not exist—yet.

Introduction: The AI Tsunami and the Question No One Is Asking

Imagine a world emerging now—not distant science fiction, but the near horizon already visible in accelerating systems and shifting workflows.

You wake not to an alarm, but to a suggestion—quiet, calibrated, almost courteous. An intelligent system already knows how well you slept, what yesterday demanded of you, and what kind of day is most likely to unfold. Breakfast requires little effort. Transportation is coordinated without friction. Messages, logistics, and schedules move into place without your direct involvement.

Much of the invisible labor that once filled human lives now happens quietly in the background—handled by machines that do not tire, forget, or ask for more time.

For some, this world feels like liberation.
For others, it feels deeply unsettling.

Work—at least as previous generations understood it—has begun to loosen its grip on daily life. Roles that once anchored identity have thinned or vanished, automated away not through malice, but through efficiency. New forms of work have emerged just as quickly, but they demand different capacities: judgment instead of repetition, creativity instead of compliance, wisdom instead of speed.

Some people move easily into this transition.
Others feel as though the ground shifted while they were standing still.

This is not speculation.
It is the direction of travel—already underway.

Artificial intelligence is no longer a future technology waiting to arrive. It is a present force—reshaping how value is created, how decisions are made, and how human effort is measured. Productivity gains that once unfolded over decades now arrive within a single career. Tasks that defined entire professions are increasingly completed in moments. The pace of change itself has become the defining challenge.

Few public figures have spoken about this acceleration as plainly as Elon Musk. Across electric vehicles, space exploration, artificial intelligence, robotics, and neural interfaces, he has returned to a single claim:

humanity is approaching a civilizational threshold. A world of unprecedented abundance. A world in which machines perform most economically necessary labor. A world in which human beings are freed—perhaps for the first time in history—to confront a deeper question.

Not how we will work—
but why.

Musk is not the only voice shaping this future, nor is he infallible. But his willingness to speak candidly about acceleration, disruption, and meaning—and, more importantly, his actions in building toward it—makes his perspective a useful lens. He describes a trajectory toward post-scarcity provision, where survival is no longer mediated by employment and material needs are increasingly automated. His repeated emphasis on universal high income as functional infrastructure underscores the shift: work becomes optional, and abundance becomes the baseline.

In such a world, the greatest risk is not mass unemployment.
It is mass disorientation.

We are already seeing the early signs. Entry-level roles that once trained generations are thinning. Routine cognitive work is increasingly automated. At the same time, new roles are emerging around human–AI collaboration, system oversight, ethics, governance, and creative synthesis.

Most jobs are not disappearing outright.
They are being reshaped—compressed around responsibility rather than repetition.

The value of a human being is no longer defined primarily by how much they can produce.
It is defined by what only a human can contribute.

This transition is not evenly distributed, and it is not emotionally neutral. Technology evolves faster than culture adapts. Systems can update overnight; identities cannot. For generations, work has been more than income—it has been structure, status, and story. As AI absorbs more of what humans once did to justify their place in the world, many will feel unmoored—even in the midst of abundance.

That is where this book begins.

I, AI: Preparing for Tomorrow's Jobs in the Musk Era is not a technical manual and not a manifesto against automation. It is a book about orientation—intellectual, practical, and human. Drawing from current AI capabilities, economic shifts, and the acceleration mindset exemplified by Musk's ventures, it explores how work is changing, which roles are emerging, and how individuals can remain relevant without becoming reactive.

The central argument is simple and enduring:

Artificial intelligence will continue to automate routine work—but it will amplify human strengths.

Judgment, empathy, creativity, leadership, and moral reasoning do not disappear in an intelligent world. They become more valuable.

The future will not belong to those who compete with machines.
It will belong to those who learn how to work with them—
and who know who they are when the work is done.

Preparation, then, is not about fear.
It is about posture.

Lifelong learning, ethical clarity, adaptability, and a renewed understanding of purpose will matter more than any single credential. The challenge ahead is not surviving the AI tsunami.

The most disruptive thing about artificial intelligence is not that it will replace human work—

but that it will finally reveal how much of our meaning was borrowed from necessity.

Before we go further, pause long enough to take stock.

AI Readiness Quiz

Score each question from 1 (not at all) to 5 (highly developed).

1. How comfortable are you using AI tools in your daily work or problem-solving?

2. Have you intentionally upskilled in adjacent areas—data literacy, systems thinking, ethics, or human-centered design—within the past year?

3. Are you building relationships in fields affected by AI?

4. How well do you adapt to change?

5. If traditional employment became optional, do you know how you would contribute

6. How strong are your "human edge" capabilities—empathy, creativity, influence, and judgment?

Scoring

Under 20: Awareness is growing, but intentional preparation is needed.

20–30: You are adapting, though gaps remain.

Over 30: You are ahead of the curve—now the focus shifts to leadership and leverage.

This score is not a verdict.
It is a starting point.

By the end of this book, you will not only understand how AI is reshaping work—you will have a framework for building a resilient, meaningful path forward in a world where intelligence is abundant and purpose is the true scarce resource.

Revisit this quiz quarterly. Note what has shifted in your role or mindset, and adjust one small practice accordingly.
(A full template appears in the Resources section.)

Orientation: Why This Book Uses the "Musk Era" Lens

This book uses the phrase *the Musk Era* deliberately—but not reverently, and not narrowly.

It does not require agreement with every statement, decision, or controversy associated with Elon Musk. Nor does it suggest that one individual determines the future alone. The phrase names a pattern of execution that has become impossible to ignore.

While the Musk-era posture—spanning physical manufacturing, energy, robotics, neural interfaces, and cognitive systems—provides a uniquely clarifying example of acceleration treated as architectural reality rather than debate, parallel trajectories reinforce the same underlying dynamics. Labs pursuing aggressive scaling of frontier models, organizations building vertically integrated AI-native workflows, and state-directed infrastructure efforts in other regions are constructing systems that assume abundance, minimize marginal human labor, and compress routine execution at unprecedented speed.

What unites these paths is not allegiance to any single figure or organization, but a shared posture: the future is being built first, and society adapts afterward.

In this sense, the Musk lens serves not as an exclusive frame, but as a particularly vivid and integrated one—exposing assumptions about necessity and meaning more starkly because it spans both the digital and physical worlds simultaneously.

Many figures speak about artificial intelligence, automation, and the future of work. Far fewer design systems as if those forces are already decisive. Fewer still build across enough domains to expose how deeply those assumptions reach.

This distinction matters.

There are other plausible lenses for understanding the AI transition. Some emphasize platform dominance and software ecosystems. Others highlight state-driven models shaped by policy and labor protection. Still others focus narrowly on AI research trajectories, abstracted from physical constraint.

Each captures part of the picture.
None captures the whole.

This book is not primarily about prediction, regulation, or innovation in isolation. It is about execution under the assumption that post-scarcity is real—and about what happens to work, identity, and meaning when systems are built as if that assumption has already crossed from theory into practice.

A Distinctive Executional Posture

Across energy, manufacturing, transportation, robotics, artificial intelligence, space systems, and neural interfaces, Musk's ventures share a consistent posture toward the future:

1. Acceleration is assumed, not debated
2. Automation is treated as default, not as a last resort
3. Human labor is minimized as infrastructure, not optimized as identity

Systems are designed to run continuously, with humans intervening selectively rather than participating proportionally

This posture is not rhetorical.
It is architectural.

Factories designed for near-zero marginal labor do not argue about the future of work—they quietly redefine it. Reusable rockets do not debate abundance—they collapse cost curves by design. Autonomous systems do not negotiate meaning—they execute objectives at scale.

What makes this lens useful is not that every outcome will unfold exactly as envisioned. It is that the direction of travel is being locked in by what is built first.

Other builders operate primarily in digital or institutional layers. This one spans the physical and cognitive world simultaneously. Energy, manufacturing, logistics, intelligence, and automation converge in a single executional portfolio. That convergence exposes assumptions about labor, value, and necessity more quickly—and more starkly—than isolated advances ever could.

In this sense, the Musk Era is not about a man.
It is about a moment.

The Conditions This Posture Creates

When systems are built from this executional posture, they begin to produce conditions—whether or not society has consciously chosen them yet.

Three conditions increasingly define this era:

1. Abundance is treated as an engineering problem, not a moral aspiration

2. Automation becomes the baseline assumption, not the exception

3. Human labor is no longer required for scale, even if human judgment remains essential

When infrastructure is built on these conditions, culture does not get to vote in advance. Society adapts after the fact. Identity lags behind execution.

That lag—not artificial intelligence itself—is the central human challenge of this era.

This book does not argue that this future will arrive evenly, cleanly, or without harm. It argues something more modest—and more urgent:

Enough of this future is already present to demand orientation.

The chapters that follow examine acceleration, job compression, hybrid roles, education, ethics, resilience, and purpose through this executional lens—not to glorify technology, but to clarify what remains human when intelligence proliferates.

The Musk Era is not about admiration or allegiance.
It is about exposure.

It reveals which assumptions about work, meaning, and identity were quietly propped up by scarcity—and which endure when scarcity begins to dissolve.

That is the ground on which this book stands.

Author's Note

Before we dive in, a word about why I'm the one writing this.

I've spent more than three decades inside education—as a coach, teacher, preK–12 school principal, and founder of a virtual school—helping learners and systems adapt when the world changed faster than institutions could. I've watched traditional models resist, then recalibrate, and I've helped build new ones when the old paths couldn't keep pace.

That experience taught me a simple truth: the future rewards those who *"skate to where the puck is going, not where it has been."*
— Wayne Gretzky

Recently, that truth became personal in an unexpected way. Three teenagers volunteered to help me move. In the course of ordinary conversation, they spoke—without prompting—about artificial intelligence, its impact on the workforce, and what it was already doing to education. They weren't repeating headlines. They were thinking strategically.

Each had made a deliberate decision to step away from traditional classrooms and into more autonomous, parent-supported learning paths. Not because they rejected learning—but because they wanted the freedom to pursue skills they believed would matter in a future that is difficult to predict. They had chosen to become autodidactic, not out of rebellion, but out of clarity.

That conversation stopped me. It forced me to ask, again, a question I've asked my entire career: Where is the puck actually going now—and how can we help people prepare for it without losing themselves along the way?

That moment clarified why this book needed to be written.

This is not a technical manual, a policy manifesto, or an alarmist warning about AI. It is orientation—from someone who has lived through disruption in learning and now sees artificial intelligence as the next inflection point, only faster and more profound.

My focus is posture: how to stay anchored in what only humans can offer—judgment, empathy, ethical direction, and purpose—while the ground shifts beneath us. If you're an autodidact, educator, professional, parent, or simply someone who can feel the acceleration, this book is written for you: to help you ride the tsunami without losing yourself.

Let's begin.

Chapter 1

The AI Tsunami—Acceleration, Compression, and the Shape of What's Coming

What remains difficult is accepting the pace.

Artificial intelligence is not advancing as a distant possibility or a speculative future. It is already reshaping workflows, condensing roles, and reorganizing value across industries. The transformation is not loud or theatrical. It is quiet, cumulative, and structural—unfolding inside systems most people interact with every day.

The relevant question is no longer whether artificial intelligence will change work.
That question has already been answered.

The question now is how fast the change is occurring—and whether human identity can recalibrate quickly enough to keep pace.

Acceleration Without Permission

Historically, major economic transitions unfolded slowly enough for institutions to adapt. Education systems retooled. Professions evolved. Cultural narratives absorbed disruption over time. Even when displacement occurred, it arrived with sufficient warning for social systems to respond.

Artificial intelligence breaks that pattern.

Productivity gains once measured across generations now arrive within a single career. Tasks that defined entire professions are increasingly handled in moments. Entry-level roles that once served as training grounds thin quietly, replaced by automation that requires supervision rather than participation.

This acceleration is not evenly distributed, and it is not emotionally neutral. Some individuals move readily into new roles shaped by judgment and synthesis. Others experience a persistent sense that the ground has shifted while they were standing still.

Compression, Not Collapse

Despite popular narratives, artificial intelligence does not eliminate work indiscriminately.
It compresses it.

Routine, repeatable, and predictable layers of labor are automated first. Execution scales. Oversight remains human. What once required teams now requires judgment. What once demanded time now demands discernment.

This pattern is already visible across domains:

- In software, build time collapses while review, integration, and responsibility expand.
- In design, drafting accelerates while intent and accountability remain human.
- In finance, analysis scales while risk tolerance and decision authority stay personal.
- In education, personalization expands while formation and meaning resist automation.

Real-world workflows increasingly reflect this compression. Administrative teams that once required multiple staff now operate with a single overseer monitoring automated flows. Content pipelines condense to one human guiding tone, context, and final responsibility. Customer support systems resolve the predictable majority automatically, leaving humans to handle trust repair and escalation.

Most jobs do not disappear outright.
They are re-formed around responsibility rather than repetition.

When Acceleration Is Built, Not Debated

Public conversation often lags behind reality. Artificial intelligence is still treated by many as a policy question or an ethical debate awaiting resolution.

Meanwhile, some actors behave as if the debate is already settled.

They do not wait for consensus.
They build.

Infrastructure shapes behavior long before culture catches up. Factories designed for near-zero marginal labor do not announce an existential shift—they simply operate. Systems that automate cognition do not argue about meaning—they execute. Once such systems are in place, society adapts not in theory, but in lived experience.

The Real Risk Ahead

The greatest risk of artificial intelligence is not technological failure.
It is human lag.

For generations, work quietly answered fundamental questions: *Who am I useful to? Where do I belong? What do I contribute?* As AI absorbs more of the routines that once answered those questions by default, humans are forced to answer them directly.

That moment is unsettling.
It is also clarifying.

Artificial intelligence does not remove purpose—it removes the illusion that purpose was being supplied automatically by necessity.

Why This Book Begins Here

This book does not begin with fear or resistance.
It begins with orientation.

Understanding the AI tsunami requires more than technical awareness. It requires recognizing how acceleration reshapes identity, how compression alters meaning, and how abundance—if it arrives unevenly—can destabilize societies long organized by necessity.

Some are already building the future as if this transition is inevitable.

The next chapter examines who they are—and what their choices reveal about what comes next.

Chapter 2

Elon Musk's Vision—What He Builds, Not What He Predicts

Elon Musk does not describe the future as a distant possibility.
He treats it as a trajectory—and then begins constructing systems that assume it is already underway.

This is what distinguishes Musk from most public commentators on artificial intelligence and the future of work. Many speak about acceleration. Few act as if it is already real. Musk's argument is not primarily rhetorical. It is infrastructural.

To understand why his perspective matters, it is not enough to quote what he has said. It is necessary to examine what he has built—and what those systems quietly assume about the world they are entering.

Abundance as an Engineering Constraint

Across Musk's ventures, scarcity is not treated as an inevitability to manage.
It is treated as a problem to eliminate.

The pattern is consistent:

1. Reduce marginal cost
2. Automate relentlessly
3. Integrate vertically
4. Scale faster than institutions adapt

Electric vehicles were not merely a shift in transportation. They were an attempt to collapse the cost curve of energy consumption and manufacturing. Reusable rockets were not simply about space exploration; they were about breaking the economics of access to orbit by removing waste from the system. Factories designed to operate continuously with minimal human intervention are not experiments—they are prototypes.

Musk does not frame abundance as a moral aspiration.
He treats it as an engineering constraint.

If scarcity can be designed out of a system, he assumes it should be.

When that assumption guides construction, the economic role of human labor begins to change—not gradually, but structurally.

The End of Work as Infrastructure

When Musk says that "most jobs will not be needed," the claim is often interpreted as a prediction of mass unemployment. That reading misses the deeper implication.

He is not describing the disappearance of effort.
He is describing the end of human labor as infrastructure.

Across manufacturing, logistics, transportation, and increasingly cognitive domains, his companies pursue environments where execution is automated and oversight is minimal. Scale no longer requires proportional human participation. Systems run continuously. Humans intervene selectively.

Humanoid robotics makes this ambition explicit. The goal is not task-specific automation, but general-purpose labor—machines capable of performing a wide range of physical work without constant human direction.

If such systems mature, the economic logic that once required millions of people to trade time for survival weakens.

Work does not vanish.
Its structural necessity does.

Intelligence Becomes Cheap—Judgment Does Not

Musk has repeatedly argued that artificial intelligence will make intelligence itself abundant and inexpensive. While often dismissed as exaggeration, his actions reveal the assumption beneath the claim.

Compute scales.
Models improve.
Automation compounds.

The cost of generating analysis, prediction, and output continues to fall.

When intelligence becomes cheap, it stops functioning as a differentiator.

What grows scarce instead is judgment: deciding what should be optimized, what should be restrained, and which consequences are acceptable. Machines execute objectives. They do not choose values. Machines scale power. They do not carry moral responsibility for outcomes.

This is why Musk returns—sometimes awkwardly—to questions of alignment and safety. He recognizes that capability without direction magnifies harm as efficiently as benefit.

Yet the systems he builds primarily solve for scale.
The unresolved space is human.

Universal Provision and the Meaning Gap

Musk's support for some form of universal income follows naturally from this worldview. If labor is no longer the primary gateway to survival, provision must be decoupled from employment. Income becomes infrastructure—stabilizing the transition while automation accelerates.

Such systems may reduce fear and soften displacement.
They may even expand freedom.
They do not supply purpose.

What Musk Reveals—Whether He Intends To or Not

The significance of Musk's work is not that he predicts the future correctly in every detail. It is that his actions consistently arrive before culture, education, and identity structures have adjusted.

He builds first.
Society reacts later.

Factories operate with fewer people.
Software replaces layers of cognitive labor.
Robots move from novelty to inevitability.

Institutions then scramble to explain what still matters.

In this way, Musk functions less as a prophet than as a stress test. His ventures expose which assumptions about work, value, and identity were quietly propped up by scarcity—and which endure when scarcity begins to dissolve.

A Note on Converging Trajectories

While Musk's portfolio offers one of the most visible and integrated examples of this executional posture, parallel patterns are emerging elsewhere: aggressive frontier-model scaling that drives intelligence toward commodity pricing, vertically integrated AI-native platforms that compress cognitive workflows, and large-scale infrastructure projects—both private and state-directed—that treat abundance as a solvable engineering challenge rather than a distant aspiration.

These paths, though different in architecture, converge on the same structural realities:

1. Automation as default
2. Labor as non-proportional to scale
3. Judgment as the remaining human constraint

The Musk lens is therefore not exclusive, but particularly revealing because it bridges physical and cognitive domains simultaneously.

The Question That Follows

If this trajectory proves even partially correct, humanity is not facing the end of work so much as the end of work as a default meaning-generator.

Execution scales.
Provision stabilizes.
Intelligence proliferates.

What remains unresolved is direction.

That is the space this book occupies.

Not how to compete with machines, but how to orient yourself when machines handle much of what once structured life. Not how to preserve disappearing roles, but how to cultivate judgment, responsibility, and contribution when necessity no longer assigns them by default.

Musk shows us where the puck is going—not by saying it, but by skating there first.

What remains is the harder task: deciding who we become when we arrive.

Chapter 3

How AI Touches Work—A Sector-Level Orientation (Not a Forecast)

Artificial intelligence is often discussed in terms of jobs lost or jobs created. That framing misses the deeper truth.

AI does not eliminate professions.
It eliminates unexamined tasks within professions.

Across analyses from institutions such as the World Economic Forum, McKinsey Global Institute, and others, the global picture is consistent:

1. Tens of millions of roles will be disrupted by 2030
2. A similar number of new roles will emerge
3. Hundreds of millions of workers will experience task-level change, not instant replacement

What follows is not a prediction of winners and losers. It is a map—showing where AI absorbs routine work, where it amplifies human judgment, and where identity—not employment—faces the greatest strain.

Technology and Software

What AI absorbs

Routine coding, testing, debugging, documentation, and data processing—especially at the entry level.

What changes

Developers shift from writing code to designing systems, integrating AI, validating outputs, and exercising architectural judgment. The locus of value moves up the abstraction stack.

By 2025–2026, agentic coding assistants and multi-step reasoning workflows have compressed junior and mid-level implementation time significantly in many teams, accelerating the shift toward system design and oversight.

What grows

AI integration specialists, system designers, ethicists, and builders who translate human intent into machine execution.

Human implication
The bottleneck is no longer syntax.
It is thinking clearly about complex systems.

Healthcare

What AI absorbs
Documentation, scheduling, image analysis, pattern recognition, and routine diagnostics.

What changes
Clinicians spend less time feeding systems and more time interpreting, deciding, and caring. AI becomes a second set of eyes—not a replacement for judgment.

Frontier models now routinely match or exceed human baselines in radiology detection and early pathology screening (2025–2026 deployments), allowing specialists to focus on complex differentials, patient communication, and ethical tradeoffs.

What grows
Care coordinators, technicians, AI-augmented clinicians, and roles supporting aging populations.

Human implication
Healthcare becomes more human as machines carry the clerical weight.

Manufacturing

What AI absorbs

Repetitive assembly, quality inspection, and predictable manual processes.

What changes

Factories shift toward oversight, maintenance, customization, and optimization. Humans supervise intelligent systems rather than replace them bolt by bolt.

What grows

Robotics technicians, AI maintenance roles, and advanced manufacturing tied to energy and infrastructure.

Human implication

The value of work shifts from endurance to situational awareness.

Administrative and Office Support

What AI absorbs

Scheduling, data entry, reporting, basic coordination, and internal communication.

What changes

Many traditional clerical roles disappear entirely or

collapse into hybrid positions augmented by AI. Organizations have already reduced administrative staffing layers by 40–70 percent in some cases through integrated automation flows (2025–2026 reality).

What grows

Few direct replacements—reskilling becomes the dominant pathway forward.

Human implication

This is the clearest zone of displacement, not because the work lacks dignity, but because it was defined almost entirely by repetition.

Finance and Accounting

What AI absorbs

Bookkeeping, auditing, reconciliation, and routine analysis.

What changes

Humans move toward advisory roles, judgment, compliance, and strategy while machines handle computation at scale.

What grows

Risk management, AI-enabled financial tools, and roles blending finance with technical fluency.

Human implication
When calculation is free, wisdom becomes expensive.

Education

What AI absorbs
Grading, administrative tasks, content generation, and baseline instruction.

What changes
Education becomes more personalized and mentorship-driven. Teachers shift from content delivery to guidance, interpretation, and formation.

What grows
Learning designers, reskilling instructors, and human-centered educators.

Human implication
AI cannot replace formation.
It can only accelerate access to information.

The Pattern Beneath the Sectors

Across industries, the same forces repeat:

1. Routine tasks collapse first
2. Judgment, creativity, and responsibility rise

3. Work fragments before it disappears

4. Identity disruption precedes job loss

AI's economic impact is best understood not as mass unemployment, but as mass re-orientation.

What This Means for You

The safest skills in an AI-saturated world are not technical alone.
They are interpretive:

- Knowing what to ask
- Knowing when to trust or challenge outputs
- Knowing why something matters

The future of work will not be decided by how intelligent machines become.
It will be decided by whether humans remain intentional, grounded, and awake as intelligence becomes abundant.

Chapter 4

AI-Centric Careers—Where the Work Actually Goes

Artificial intelligence does not create opportunity evenly.
It concentrates it.

Every major technological shift produces surface-level excitement—new tools, new titles, new promises of relevance. But lasting opportunity does not emerge where attention is loudest. It gathers where infrastructure is being built and power is already accumulating.

AI is no exception.

The question is not which jobs will exist.
It is where responsibility migrates when routine execution scales.

Careers in the AI era are best understood not as isolated roles, but as positions within systems—systems designed to operate at scale with minimal human labor and maximum leverage.

When intelligence becomes abundant, work reorganizes around three structural layers.

Layer One: Capability Builders

Those who make intelligent systems function

At the base of every AI-driven ecosystem are those who build capability itself. These roles enable machines to perceive, reason, and act reliably in complex environments.

This layer includes:

- Engineers who design and refine intelligent systems
- Robotics specialists who translate software into physical action
- Model trainers and data curators who shape what systems learn

As tools mature, less effort is spent on raw invention and more on integration, reliability, and scale.

The demand here is real—but finite.
Capability building does not employ the masses.

As systems stabilize, the center of gravity moves upward.

Layer Two: Translators and Integrators

Those who make intelligence usable, safe, and effective

As AI absorbs routine execution, organizations encounter a new problem: intelligent systems rarely fail loudly. They fail subtly—through edge cases, misalignment, context loss, and unintended consequences.

This creates sustained demand for people who operate between domains.

These roles include:

- Human–AI collaboration designers
- Systems integrators who connect AI to real workflows
- Reliability, safety, and quality specialists
- Domain experts translating human intent into machine-operable constraints

This work is neither purely technical nor purely human.
It requires fluency in both.

Many integrators now routinely oversee agentic workflows—multi-step reasoning chains in frontier models—catching drift, correcting context, and ensuring alignment with human values.

A Real-World Example: The Logistics Integrator

Alex is a mid-level logistics manager at a large e-commerce fulfillment center. For years, his role involved daily manual adjustments—rerouting shipments, negotiating with carriers, balancing inventory against demand forecasts.

Then AI-driven forecasting and routing arrived. Overnight, the platform automated most routine decisions.

At first, it felt like diminishment.
Instead, his role clarified.

Alex now oversees AI outputs. When disruptions occur, he decides:

- Do we prioritize speed or cost?

- Do we override for ethical sourcing?
- Do we accept risk to honor a delivery promise?

Execution compressed.
Responsibility concentrated.

Alex's value now lies not in moving shipments, but in deciding which tradeoffs are acceptable.

Layer Three: Stewards and Governors

Those who decide how power is used

As AI-driven systems scale, stewardship becomes unavoidable. Power concentrates before meaning catches up.

These roles include:

- Alignment specialists
- Ethics and governance leaders
- Oversight and audit roles
- Policy translators between technical systems and institutions

Stewardship does not scale the way automation does. It relies on judgment, moral reasoning, and responsibility—qualities that cannot be delegated without erosion of trust.

As AI becomes more powerful, this layer becomes more, not less, valuable.

Why These Roles Persist

What unites these layers is not technical novelty.
It is responsibility density.

As execution becomes cheap, the human work that remains is the work that carries consequence.

Credentials matter less than posture.
Adaptability matters more than specialization.

The most durable roles are not the most glamorous.
They are the ones closest to power—and therefore requiring restraint.

Finding Your Place in the System

Rather than asking which job titles will exist, better questions emerge:

1. Where is intelligence already deployed at scale?

2. Which parts of that system still require human

judgment?

3. Where does failure carry real consequence?

Career Alignment Exercise

- Identify which layer draws you most: builder, integrator, or steward
- Assess where your current skills translate across domains
- Choose one experiment that increases proximity to responsibility

Map yourself here:

Base: Capability Builders (technical scale)

Middle: Translators and Integrators (hybrid fluency)

Top: Stewards and Governors (judgment and direction)

Do not chase the gold rush.
Position yourself near the infrastructure.

That is where work persists when automation scales—and where meaning survives when necessity fades.

Chapter 5

Human–AI Hybrids—Where Empathy Wins

Artificial intelligence excels at pattern recognition, prediction, and scale.
It does not excel at presence.

As intelligent systems absorb mechanical and cognitive routines, differentiation shifts. Value migrates away from efficiency alone and toward capacities that require human judgment, trust, and relational accountability.

This is not a sentimental claim.
It is an economic one.

When execution becomes cheap, what cannot be automated becomes scarce. In intelligent systems, empathy, continuity, and ethical responsibility do not disappear—they concentrate.

Healthcare: Trust as the Differentiator

AI increasingly assists with diagnostics, imaging analysis, and treatment planning—often with speed and accuracy beyond human baselines. These tools matter. They improve outcomes, reduce error, and expand access.

Yet healing itself remains relational.

Patients do not experience care as a dataset. They experience fear, uncertainty, vulnerability, and hope. Clinicians integrate AI insight with context—values, family dynamics, ethical tradeoffs—prioritizing dignity alongside data.

The more medicine is optimized, the more human presence differentiates it.

Trust becomes the scarce resource.
Trust is not automated.

A Real-World Observation: Continuity Under Pressure

During a prolonged hospital stay involving advanced care, I witnessed a pattern that technology alone could not resolve.

Clinical teams were skilled, compassionate, and diligent. Yet frequent handoffs—inevitable in modern healthcare—meant that context had to be re-established repeatedly. Decisions were often correct, but continuity was fragile.

This was not a failure of competence.
It was a structural limitation.

Imagine instead an always-on intelligence layer—a persistent AI system that maintains longitudinal memory: treatment history, prior decisions, evolving context, and unresolved questions. Not a replacement for clinicians, but a stabilizing presence beneath them.

The AI carries memory.
Humans carry responsibility.

In such a system, judgment, empathy, and ethical reasoning become more central—not less. AI absorbs the burden of recall and coordination so clinicians can focus on interpretation, trust, and care.

Education: Formation Resists Automation

Intelligent systems personalize instruction, generate content, and compress administrative work. These capabilities expand access and efficiency.

What does not automate is formation.

As tools absorb logistics, educators move into hybrid roles—guiding reflection, cultivating curiosity, modeling judgment, and mentoring students through uncertainty. Instruction scales. Influence deepens.

Teaching remains an act of relationship.

The more content delivery accelerates, the more essential human presence becomes.

Leadership: Influence Is Not Computational

AI informs decisions.
It does not persuade people to carry them out.

Leadership is relational. It is the work of aligning people, reconciling values, and assuming responsibility for consequences—especially when outcomes are uncertain or costly.

As decision support scales, accountability intensifies. Leaders cannot delegate moral weight to systems without eroding trust.

Leadership roles do not shrink in intelligent systems. They become more demanding.

Hybrid Roles as the Center of Gravity

Human–AI hybrid roles are not consolation prizes. They are the center of gravity.

Machines provide leverage.
Humans provide direction.

As systems optimize execution, responsibility concentrates in those who decide when to intervene, when to override, and when to restrain.

Empathy, judgment, and presence must be chosen and cultivated in an optimized world. They do not survive acceleration by accident.

Chapter 6

New Frontiers: Space, Sustainability, and the Next Human Horizon

Artificial intelligence does not advance in isolation.

As intelligent systems scale, they intersect with humanity's oldest ambitions: exploration, preservation, and transcendence. AI does more than optimize existing industries. It opens domains that were previously unreachable—too complex, too distant, or too fragile for sustained human effort alone.

When machines assume much of the labor required for survival, humanity is freed—sometimes uncomfortably—to confront a deeper question:

What is worth building next?

Space as a Test Case

Space exploration offers the clearest illustration of this shift.

Autonomous systems already navigate hostile environments, analyze terrain, and coordinate logistics beyond real-time human control. Intelligent agents correct trajectories, manage power systems, and operate where delay makes direct oversight impossible.

Yet the most important work in space is not computational.

Designing off-world habitats requires more than engineering. It demands psychology, biology, ethics, and foresight—creating environments that sustain not only life, but human dignity. Expansion without restraint risks exporting Earth's extractive habits into irreversible contexts.

Current missions already reflect this hybrid reality. Autonomous systems handle scale—navigation, data collection, and optimization—while human teams interpret anomalies, weigh ethical tradeoffs, and decide which outcomes are acceptable.

Here, the human edge is responsibility.

Space is not merely a destination.
It is a mirror.

It reveals what values we carry when constraints fall away.

Sustainability: Repair at Planetary Scale

If space represents expansion outward, sustainability represents repair inward.

Intelligent systems now model climate dynamics, optimize energy networks, and predict environmental shifts at scales no human team could manage. Algorithms identify efficiencies that reduce waste and emissions.

These tools matter.
They buy time.

But sustainability is not a technical problem alone.
It is a moral commitment.

Decisions about tradeoffs—growth versus restraint, speed versus care, profit versus preservation—cannot be delegated to machines without hollowing responsibility. AI supplies leverage. Humans supply values.

Across sustainability efforts, a consistent pattern is emerging: data-heavy layers compress, while human judgment concentrates. Predictive models inform decisions, but stewards integrate those forecasts with local knowledge, long-term impact, and ethical limits.

Repair at planetary scale requires knowing when *not* to optimize—as much as knowing how.

The Intimate Frontier: Human Augmentation

Beyond planet and environment lies the most delicate frontier of all: the human body and mind.

Neural interfaces, cognitive augmentation, and longevity research promise expanded capacity and restored function. For those living with impairment or neurological injury, these advances offer genuine hope.

Yet they also raise questions that capability alone cannot answer.

Where does enhancement end and identity begin?
What happens when performance outpaces wisdom?
Who bears responsibility when boundaries blur?

These are not questions of speed.
They are questions of meaning.

As augmentation advances, AI increases capacity—but human oversight remains essential to preserve agency, dignity, and alignment with values. Power over the self cannot be optimized without consequence.

The Pattern Across Frontiers

Across these domains—space, sustainability, and augmentation—the pattern holds:

AI extends reach.
Humans decide direction.
Power without orientation magnifies consequence.

The more intelligence scales, the more deliberate humanity must become.

Chapter 7

Essential Skills in an Accelerating World—Adaptability Over Expertise

For much of modern history, expertise functioned as professional armor. You learned a domain, mastered its rules, and relied on that mastery for stability.

Artificial intelligence changes this equation.

When intelligent systems retrieve, synthesize, and generate knowledge instantly, static expertise depreciates faster than ever. What once protected now constrains. Mastery that cannot be revised becomes friction rather than leverage.

The future will not belong to those who know the most.
It will belong to those who learn the fastest—and integrate what they learn wisely.

Redefining Intelligence

As AI absorbs pattern recognition and routine analysis, the human role shifts.

Analysis gives way to synthesis: the ability to integrate information across domains, weigh tradeoffs, and determine what matters when everything is available. Influence evolves as well. Leadership no longer depends on controlling information, but on aligning people and systems around shared purpose.

These are not soft skills.
They are survival skills.

In intelligent environments, value concentrates around those who can connect ideas, interpret consequences, and guide direction under uncertainty.

Lifelong Learning as Discipline

Lifelong learning is often framed as curiosity or openness. In practice, it is a discipline.

It requires rhythm, selectivity, and humility—the willingness to revise assumptions as conditions change. Adaptability is not chaos. It is coherence under revision.

Those who adapt well do not chase novelty. They test ideas in context, retain what compounds, and discard what does not. The goal is not constant reinvention, but continuous alignment.

Learning shifts from accumulation to integration.

The Cost of Static Expertise

When identity is fused to a single role or domain, change feels like erasure.
When identity is anchored in values and direction, change becomes translation.

The work shifts.
The purpose holds.

From leading schools through technological and structural transitions, the pattern was consistent. Educators who clung to "how we've always done it" struggled most. Those who reframed their role around synthesis, relational formation, and ethical guidance adapted fastest—and often became guides for others navigating the transition.

Static expertise resists revision.
Adaptive expertise absorbs it.

Adaptability Skills Audit

To assess your readiness, rate yourself from **1 (low)** to **5 (high)** on the following capacities:

- **Synthesis** — integrating insights across domains
- **Influence** — aligning people and systems around shared purpo
- **Lifelong learning** — updating models and assumptions rhythmical
- **Ethical discernment** — weighing values as capability scales
- **Curiosity** — openness to emergent patterns without defensiveness

Identify one area where expertise has become static rather than generative.

Commit to one adaptive practice for the next 30 days. Examples include:

1. Reading across disciplines and prompting a frontier model to help surface tensions and synthesize pers
2. Building a small prototype that blends human judgment with AI leverage (for example, using

multi-step reasoning agents to explore trade-offs in a real decision

3. Mentoring someone through a transition in your field

4. Experimenting in an unfamiliar domain with deliberate reflectio

The Adaptation Loop

Adaptability is not a one-time upgrade. It is a repeating cycle:

1. **Observe** — gather new inputs through tools, experience, and dialogue

2. **Integrate** — synthesize with existing models; discard what no longer fits

3. **Apply** — test in real context through a project, decision, or conversation

4. **Reflect** — retain what compounds; refine what does not

Repeat this loop with increasing rhythm and depth.

Revisit this audit quarterly. Document one discarded assumption or newly integrated insight, and adjust accordingly.

In a world where tools evolve rapidly, adaptability compounds faster than mastery.

Those who learn to revise without losing themselves do more than keep pace.
They preserve continuity of purpose in the midst of change.

That continuity—not static expertise—is what allows human judgment to endure as intelligence becomes abundant.

Chapter 8

Education and Upskilling—From Degrees to Discernment

For generations, education followed a predictable arc. You studied early, specialized midstream, and relied on that foundation for decades. Credentials signaled readiness. Degrees implied durability.

Artificial intelligence disrupts this pattern—not by making education irrelevant, but by changing how relevance is sustained.

Learning no longer ends.

As intelligent systems evolve continuously, so must the people who work alongside them. Knowledge that once carried value for a lifetime now depreciates within years—sometimes faster. What matters is no longer how much you have learned, but how well your learning compounds.

The Shift from Credentials to Capacity

Degrees still provide depth, community, and intellectual formation. They are not obsolete. But they are no longer sufficient on their own.

Increasingly, competence is demonstrated through portfolios, projects, and outcomes rather than transcripts alone. Micro-credentials, bootcamps, apprenticeships, and self-directed learning paths have emerged not as replacements, but as supplements—signals of applied capability rather than institutional passage.

This shift democratizes access.
It also introduces noise.

Not all learning compounds. Not every credential carries weight. Discernment becomes as important as diligence. The central question is no longer *"Where did you study?"* but *"What can you build, explain, or steward responsibly?"*

Across fields once gated by formal degrees, employers increasingly prioritize demonstrated synthesis—work that blends technical fluency with judgment, ethics, and context. Adaptive capacity, not static certification, is becoming the strongest predictor of sustained relevance.

Learning That Compounds

Sustainable learning shares several traits:

- It is applied rather than abstract
- It connects across domains rather than narrowing prematurely
- It produces artifacts—systems, insights, relationships—that persist beyond the course itself

In an AI-rich world, learning must also be rhythmic. Short, focused bursts of acquisition followed by periods of application allow knowledge to integrate rather than accumulate unused.

This cadence prevents both stagnation and burnout.

Education becomes less like stockpiling.
And more like cultivation.

The Role of Institutions

Institutions face their own adaptation challenge.

Schools, universities, and training organizations must move from gatekeeping to guidance—helping learners navigate abundance rather than ration scarcity.

The most effective institutions will be those that teach *how to learn*, not merely *what to know*.

From my experience founding and leading learning models through past disruptions, I've seen institutions thrive when they prioritize discernment—guiding learners to curate paths that compound human strengths rather than defending outdated structures.

For individuals, the implication is clear:

Education is no longer something you complete.
It is something you practice.

Upskilling Roadmap

To orient your learning intentionally:

1. Identify skill gaps tied to adaptability rather than prestige—synthesis, ethical reasoning, systems awareness

2. Choose two or three learning paths that reinforce one another

3. Define short-term applications—projects, experiments, or contributions that test integratio

4. Review quarterly, keeping what compounds and discarding what does not

Visualize your roadmap as a compounding spiral:

- **Acquire** — focused input through courses, tools, or experien
- **Apply** — real-world testing
- **Reflect & Refine** — discard what doesn't compound, retain what integrates

Revisit this roadmap quarterly. Document one completed application and one discarded element.

Chapter 9

Mindset and Resilience—Thriving in Uncertainty

Technical competence can open doors.
It cannot stabilize identity.

As artificial intelligence reshapes work and accelerates change, external structures grow less reliable. Roles shift. Organizations reconfigure. Uncertainty becomes the background state rather than a temporary phase.

In this environment, resilience is not a personality trait.
It is an operating system.

Living With Permanent Uncertainty

Those who struggle most are not those who lack ability, but those who require certainty in order to act.

When clarity is demanded before movement, paralysis follows.

Resilience begins with a shift in posture: treating uncertainty as information rather than threat. Change becomes something to interpret, not something to outrun.

The goal is not control.
It is orientation.

Emotional Agility and Identity

Acceleration pressures identity in subtle ways. When work shifts beneath you, loss often precedes opportunity. Ignoring that response does not build resilience.

It erodes it.

Emotional agility allows discomfort without surrendering direction. It acknowledges fear without allowing fear to dictate posture. This capacity distinguishes endurance from avoidance.

Resilient individuals do not numb themselves to disruption.
They metabolize it.

They feel dislocation without fragmentation.
They adapt without abandoning coherence.

Purpose as Anchor

In volatile environments, purpose functions as ballast. It does not remove uncertainty, but it keeps movement oriented.

When roles dissolve, purpose does not disappear.
It translates.

This is why individuals anchored in values adapt more readily than those anchored in titles. The work changes. The direction holds.

Across periods of disruption—technological shifts, institutional collapse, personal upheaval—those who framed identity around contribution rather than position maintained coherence even as external structures dissolved.

Purpose is not certainty about outcomes.
It is clarity about direction.

Chapter 10

Economic Shifts: Abundance, Inequality, and the Question of Distribution

Artificial intelligence does not merely change how people work.
It changes why economies exist.

For most of human history, economic systems have been organized around scarcity. Labor mediated access to food, shelter, security, and status. Work was not simply a means of contribution; it was the gate through which survival passed.

Artificial intelligence weakens that gate.

As intelligent systems absorb increasing amounts of economically necessary labor, the relationship between work and livelihood loosens. Abundance becomes technically possible even as traditional employment contracts.

This creates both promise and peril.

The End of Scarcity—and the Beginning of Choice

In a world where productivity scales without proportional human input, material scarcity becomes less dominant. Goods and services trend toward lower cost. Basic needs become easier to meet.

This is the optimistic arc often emphasized by technologists.

But abundance does not automatically produce equity.

Without intentional design, gains concentrate. Ownership of systems matters more than participation in labor. Those who control infrastructure capture outsized value, while those displaced by automation experience uncertainty—not only economic, but existential.

The risk is not that abundance fails to arrive.
The risk is that it arrives unevenly.

Current transitions already reveal this pattern. In administrative services, content moderation, and routine customer support, automation has compressed headcount by half or more in many organizations. Routine queries are resolved by agents. Data processing scales. Productivity rises while value flows upward—to capital, platforms, and oversight roles.

Universal Provision—and Its Limits

Proposals such as universal high income emerge naturally in this context.

By decoupling survival from employment, income floors can stabilize transitions, reduce fear-driven resistance to automation, and increase flexibility. Early experiments suggest improvements in well-being, psychological security, and even entrepreneurial activity during periods of displacement.

Yet income alone does not resolve meaning.

A society can meet material needs and still fracture internally if individuals lack pathways for meaningful contribution. Boredom, disorientation, and loss of dignity are not eliminated by abundance.

They are often intensified by it.

Contribution in a Post-Work Economy

If work becomes optional, contribution becomes intentional.

Economies must evolve to recognize and reward stewardship, care, creativity, governance, and continuity—forms of value that stabilize systems, preserve trust, and shape long-term outcomes, yet often resist easy quantification.

Early cooperative and employee-owned, AI-augmented ventures are already experimenting with contribution dividends—mechanisms that reward relational oversight, ethical alignment, community-building, and long-horizon thinking alongside traditional output.

These models suggest a path in which abundance enables broader participation rather than narrower concentration.

This shift requires more than policy.
It requires cultural reorientation.

Education must prepare individuals not just for employment, but for responsibility. Institutions must prioritize long-term contribution over short-term metrics. Systems must reward those who carry ethical direction when execution scales.

Economic Resilience Reflection

To examine your own position:

- Assess how dependent your identity and stability are on traditional labor structur
- Consider how abundance might alter your sense of purpose
- Commit to one action this quarter that builds agency beyond employment—learning a stewardship skill, mentoring across domains, creating open-value work, experimenting with cooperative models, or advocating for equitable mechanisms

Visualize your position on this contribution spectrum:

Left: Necessity-driven (survival tied to paid labor)

Center: Transition (provision decoupling, contribution emerging)

Right: Intentional (chosen stewardship and meaning)

Plot where you are now—and identify one concrete step toward the right.

Revisit this reflection quarterly. Document progress on your action, any shift in dependence or purpose clarity, and one new insight from the experiment. A full template with examples appears in the Resources section at the back of this book.

Abundance without purpose breeds fragility. Abundance oriented toward contribution builds resilience.

Chapter 11

Ethics and Policy—Steering the AI Revolution

Artificial intelligence does not arrive neutral.
It reflects the values, assumptions, and incentives of those who design and deploy it.

As capability scales, so does consequence.

Ethics and policy are not brakes on progress.
They are steering mechanisms.

Without them, acceleration magnifies harm as efficiently as benefit.

Power, Bias, and Responsibility

AI systems inherit bias from data, objectives, and structure. When deployed at scale, these biases shape access to opportunity, amplify inequity, and concentrate power—often invisibly.

The more seamless systems become, the harder their influence is to detect.

This is not a hypothetical risk.
It is an ongoing reality.

Responsibility does not disappear as systems become autonomous.
It shifts upward—to designers, operators, institutions, and policymakers.

Someone always defines objectives.
Someone determines acceptable tradeoffs.
Someone bears moral weight for outcomes.

Governance in Motion

Traditional regulatory models struggle with technologies that evolve faster than legislative cycles. Static rules fail in dynamic systems.

Effective governance must therefore be adaptive—principle-driven rather than prescriptive, iterative rather than final.

This demands new roles: alignment specialists, auditors, oversight bodies, and leaders capable of translating between technical capability and human consequence.

The tension between speed and stewardship is unavoidable.

Move too slowly, and innovation stagnates.
Move too quickly, and trust erodes.

The task is not to eliminate this tension, but to hold it responsibly.

Organizations already experimenting with iterative audits, red-teaming, and early alignment checks are discovering a critical truth: governance works best when treated as ongoing stewardship, not one-time compliance.

Ethics as Daily Practice

Ethics is often framed as abstraction—guidelines, frameworks, and statements.

In reality, it is lived in daily decisions: what to automate, what to preserve, where to intervene, and when to stop.

Every deployment is a moral act.

In an intelligent world, ethics cannot be outsourced to policy alone. It must be embodied by individuals who understand both power and consequence.

This is why ethical literacy becomes a core competency—not a niche specialization.

Ethics Reflection

To orient yourself within this responsibility:

- Assess your awareness of AI-related risks in your field—bias, power concentration, unintended optimization
- Identify one ethical concern that feels unresolved or under-discussed
- Commit to a concrete action: deeper learning, dialogue, restraint in design, or advocacy for transparency

Use this stewardship triangle as a diagnostic:

1. **Capability** — what systems can do
2. **Consequence** — what outcomes follow
3. **Values** — what should be prioritized

Identify which vertex currently needs strengthening.

The future will not be shaped solely by what artificial intelligence can do.
It will be shaped by what humans decide it *should* do.

Chapter 12

Conclusion: Your AI Future—A Blueprint for Meaning in an Intelligent World

This book began with acceleration.

Artificial intelligence is advancing faster than culture can adapt. Work is compressing. Roles are shifting. Systems are scaling before identities can catch up. The evidence is no longer speculative.

It is present. It is cumulative.

But acceleration does not dictate destiny.

One pattern has held steady across every chapter: artificial intelligence reshapes work without replacing what makes it meaningful. It automates execution. It amplifies leverage. It exposes—rather than erases—the human core.

What disappears is not purpose. What disappears is the illusion that purpose can be outsourced to necessity.

For much of modern history, survival answered the question of meaning by default. You worked because you had to. You specialized because stability demanded it. You built identity around roles because roles structured life.

Artificial intelligence weakens those structures—not to impoverish humanity, but to reveal what remains when they fall away.

That revelation is uncomfortable. It is also an invitation.

The future belongs neither to those who resist intelligent systems nor to those who surrender agency to them. It belongs to those who learn to work with machines while staying anchored in values that machines cannot create.

A Five-Part Blueprint

To move forward with intention rather than reaction, return to these five orienting commitments. They are not one-time steps, but living practices—meant to be revisited as the world continues to change.

1. **Assess Exposure and Strengths:** Map where your work intersects with automation and where it depends on judgment, responsibility, and presence. Let go of dissolving tasks without defensiveness. Reinvest in capacities that compound over time.

2. **Commit to Lifelong Learning:** Make learning rhythmic, applied, and selective. Update mental models regularly. Keep what integrates. Discard what no longer does. Learning is no longer preparation for life. It is participation in it.

3. **Cultivate a Resilient Mindset:** Uncertainty is not a phase to escape. It is the condition to inhabit. Build curiosity, emotional agility, and clarity of purpose before pressure forces the issue.

4. **Build Networks of Meaning:** No one adapts alone. Surround yourself with people who think across boundaries, carry real ethical weight, and resist both panic and complacency. In complex systems, trust scales more slowly than technology. But it scales deeper.

5. **Innovate with Purpose:** Act. Test. Contribute. Define success not only by efficiency or out-

put, but by the human flourishing your work enables.

Power requires direction. Abundance requires stewardship.

These commitments do not deliver certainty. They deliver orientation.

Beyond the Age of Necessity

If artificial intelligence delivers even a fraction of its promised potential, humanity will enter an era without precedent—one in which survival is increasingly automated and meaning must be chosen deliberately.

That is not a technological problem. It is a human one.

The question is not whether machines will become more capable. They will.

The question is whether human beings will become more responsible—more attentive to purpose, more deliberate in contribution, more rooted in values that outlast any tool.

The AI tsunami is not something to outrun. It is something to ride—with awareness, humility, and agency.

The future is not written by algorithms alone. It is shaped by the people who decide what intelligence is for.

When intelligence is everywhere, what will matter most is not what machines can do— but what humans decide is worth doing at all.

Chapter 13

Resources: Orientation Tools for an Intelligent Future

These are not required reading. They are companions—selective anchors for clear thinking, continuous learning, and staying grounded as artificial intelligence reshapes work, identity, and contribution.

Curate ruthlessly. What compounds for you will endure.

Books on AI, Abundance, and the Future of Work

These titles ground acceleration in enduring human realities—judgment, ethics, purpose, and stewardship—without chasing hype.

Co-Intelligence: Living and Working with AI — Ethan Mollick A practical guide to treating AI as collaborator—co-worker, coach, and thinking partner.

Centers human judgment, creativity, and responsibility in hybrid workflows.

Abundance — Ezra Klein & Derek Thompson Explores how innovation, infrastructure, and policy can move societies toward abundance—aligning with post-scarcity trajectories and the decoupling of survival from labor.

The Alignment Problem — Brian Christian A deeply human examination of how values, incentives, and misalignment emerge inside intelligent systems—and why ethics must be deliberately designed rather than assumed.

Superintelligence — Nick Bostrom A foundational analysis of AI trajectories, alignment challenges, and high-stakes strategic choices that could define humanity's future—essential for thinking about direction, not just capability.

The Precipice — Toby Ord A sober assessment of existential risks, including advanced AI, and humanity's responsibility to steward powerful technologies wisely—echoing this book's emphasis on stewardship over speed.

Timeless Thinkers on Work, Meaning, and Purpose

These works address the book's central question: what remains—and what must be chosen—when necessity no longer structures life?

Man's Search for Meaning — Viktor Frankl Foundational on purpose as deliberate choice rather than default provision—especially relevant when work ceases to function as the automatic meaning-generator.

The Human Condition — Hannah Arendt Distinguishes labor (necessity), work (creation), and action (public contribution), clarifying the transition from survival-bound systems to intentional stewardship.

Flow: The Psychology of Optimal Experience — Mihaly Csikszentmihalyi Explores intrinsic motivation and deep engagement—the human edge that endures in an increasingly optimized world.

Podcasts and Long-Form Conversations

Listen rhythmically—perhaps one episode per week—to stay oriented without overload.

The Ezra Klein Show Thoughtful interviews on AI, abundance agendas, societal trade-offs, and meaning—balancing optimism with institutional realism.

Lex Fridman Podcast (select AI-focused episodes) Extended conversations with builders and thinkers on intelligence, alignment, and human futures—useful for long-view posture.

AI and the Future of Work (Dan Turchin) Explores AI's impact on workplaces, ethics, and the human side of transformation—particularly strong on hybrid roles.

Latent Space: The AI Engineer Podcast Deep dives into engineering patterns, human–AI collaboration, and practical integration—valuable for builders and stewards who prefer substance over trends.

Courses and Platforms for Lifelong Learning

Prioritize rhythmic, applied paths that compound judgment and adaptability.

Coursera / edX / Udacity Begin with non-technical foundations such as *AI for Everyone* (Andrew Ng) to build AI literacy, systems awareness, and collaboration fluency. Supplement with ethics or human-centered design.

fast.ai Hands-on, accessible courses designed to get learners building quickly—emphasizing intuition, experimentation, and applied insight without heavy mathematical prerequisites.

MIT OpenCourseWare Free courses on AI, ethics, systems thinking, and societal impacts—valuable for grounding technical progress in broader human context.

World Economic Forum — Future of Jobs Reports High-level overviews of skill shifts, job compression, and labor transitions in AI-enabled economies—use for pattern recognition, not precise forecasting.

Organizations and Frameworks

Jobs for the Future (JFF) Research and frameworks focused on human-centered workforce redesign and AI-ready skills—particularly strong on hybrid roles and equitable transitions.

Online discourse communities Engage in thoughtful, cross-disciplinary conversations on X (@learningengpub) or curated forums focused on human–AI collaboration rather than hype. Share reflections, experiments, or audits—we orient together.

Tools and Practices (Practical Tie-Ins)

Daily or weekly AI experimentation Low-stakes practice with generative tools builds fluency and discernment—not dependence. Begin with prompts tied to the book's exercises (e.g., "Reframe this task to emphasize the human edge.")

Prompt libraries and collaboration frameworks Use academic and open repositories to structure AI as a collaborator in writing, planning, and problem-solving—always amplifying, never replacing, your judgment.

Quarterly personal audits Revisit the book's quizzes, reflections, and frameworks. Track posture over time:

1. What increased in responsibility density?
2. What compounded in purpose?

Use the appendix templates to log progress.

Final Note

Resources do not replace responsibility. They illuminate it.

The aim is not more consumption, but cultivated judgment in a world where intelligence is abundant and direction must be deliberately chosen.

Start small. Choose one book, one episode, or one practice this week. Apply it to a real reflection from these pages.

We are not racing. We are orienting—together.

Chapter 14

Glossary of Key Concepts

This glossary serves as a **quick-reference companion** to the book—clarifying the core terms that recur throughout. Each entry emphasizes enduring patterns rather than transient technical details, helping readers internalize the shift from necessity-driven work to intentional contribution in an accelerating world.

Abundance
The emerging state in which material scarcity dissolves through intelligent systems and automation, driving the marginal cost of goods, services, and production toward near-zero. Abundance shifts survival from labor-mediated necessity to automated provision—freeing humans to confront deeper questions of contribution, stewardship, and meaning, while introducing risks of unequal distribution if not intentionally guided.

Adaptability
The disciplined capacity to revise mental models, skills, and direction in response to rapid change without losing coherence or purpose. In an intelligent world, adaptability compounds faster than static expertise and increasingly determines who leads rather than merely survives—rooted in curiosity, humility, and selective integration.

Alignment
The ongoing responsibility to ensure intelligent systems pursue goals compatible with human values rather than drifting toward unintended or harmful outcomes. Alignment is not a one-time technical fix, but a moral and structural imperative that precedes and shapes capability—requiring human judgment, ethical clarity, and continuous oversight.

Augmentation
The enhancement of human capacities—cognitive, physical, or perceptual—through intelligent interfaces or systems. While augmentation promises expanded function and restored ability, it also raises questions of identity, boundaries, and responsibility. True augmentation amplifies the human edge rather than eroding it, demanding stewardship so performance serves wisdom, not the reverse.

Compression of Roles
The process by which intelligent systems automate mechanical, repetitive, and predictable layers of work, reducing the volume of execution required while concentrating human effort around judgment, oversight, discernment, ethical direction, and relational presence. Compression reshapes rather than eliminates most roles, filtering toward responsibility density.

Contribution
Intentional participation in something that matters beyond survival or economic necessity. In a post-work era, contribution becomes the primary source of dignity, agency, and social cohesion—rewarding stewardship, care, creativity, governance, and relational value that resist quantification and endure when necessity fades.

Disorientation
The widespread existential unease that arises when identity, structure, status, and story—long anchored in necessity-driven work—lag behind technological and economic reality. Mass disorientation, rather than unemployment alone, is the central risk of acceleration and must be addressed through posture, purpose clarity, and networks of meaning.

Human Edge
The irreplaceable human capacities—empathy, moral reasoning, relational presence, creativity, influence, ethical judgment, and contextual discernment—that become more valuable as intelligent systems absorb routine cognitive and mechanical tasks. The human edge is cultivated deliberately, not automatic, and forms the center of gravity in hybrid futures.

Hybrid Roles
Positions in which humans and intelligent systems collaborate: machines provide scale, speed, pattern recognition, and leverage, while humans supply direction, trust, compassion, accountability, and restraint. These roles are not transitional but structural necessities in mature intelligent ecosystems, rewarding fluency across technical and human domains.

Judgment-Centered Work
Work that relies on discernment, accountability, trade-off weighing, value alignment, and ethical direction—resilient to automation and increasingly central as routine layers compress. Judgment cannot be fully delegated; it remains the scarce resource when intelligence proliferates.

Post-Scarcity Provision
The trajectory toward automated infrastructure that

meets material needs without requiring proportional human employment, decoupling survival from labor and elevating the question of chosen purpose. Provision becomes functional infrastructure (often through universal mechanisms), while meaning and contribution must be intentionally cultivated.

Posture
The intentional stance toward acceleration: curiosity over fear, agency over reaction, humility over rigidity, and ethical clarity over complacency. Preparation is not about outrunning change, but learning to ride it with awareness, grounded values, and responsibility—determining whether intelligence serves flourishing or unintended consequence.

Purpose as Anchor
The ballast that keeps movement oriented when external structures—roles, titles, and necessity—dissolve. Anchored in values, direction, and contribution, purpose translates rather than disappears amid disruption, enabling resilience, emotional agility, and leadership in permanent uncertainty.

Resilience
An operating system for inhabiting permanent uncertainty without fragmentation—built through curiosity (treating change as information), emotional agility (ex-

periencing discomfort without derailment), purpose clarity (direction beyond role), and deliberate practice. Resilience is proactive posture, not reactive toughness, and determines longevity as external certainty erodes.

Stewardship
Responsible oversight and direction of powerful systems—intelligent, robotic, or frontier-expanding—to serve human flourishing, ethical boundaries, and long-term consequence rather than drift or harm. Stewardship is the enduring human role when execution scales; it relies on judgment, moral reasoning, and restraint that cannot be automated without loss of trust.

Universal High Income
A stabilizing form of infrastructure that decouples survival from employment in an abundance-driven economy, providing a baseline that softens displacement, reduces fear, and enables flexibility. As functional provision rather than passive stipend, it supports transition but does not supply meaning—requiring complementary pathways for intentional contribution and responsibility.

Chapter 15

About the Author

Christian A. Dickinson is the founder of **Learning Engineered Publishing®**, a family-run imprint dedicated to creating books, resources, and experiences that cultivate curiosity, resilience, purposeful growth, and anchored identity in a rapidly changing world.

A lifelong educator and builder, he has spent more than two decades as a coach, teacher, preK–12 school principal, and founder of virtual learning models—helping individuals and institutions adapt when change outpaced traditional structures. He has witnessed resistance, recalibration, and reinvention firsthand, and views artificial intelligence as the next profound inflection point: faster, broader, and more existential.

Guided by Wayne Gretzky's principle to *"skate to where the puck is going, not where it has been,"* Dickinson writes from the deep conviction that enduring relevance lies not in competing with intelligent systems, but in amplifying irreplaceable human strengths: judgment, empathy, leadership, ethical direction, and chosen purpose.

I, AI: Preparing for Tomorrow's Jobs in the Musk Era emerges from this perspective—an orientation guide for riding acceleration without losing oneself, and for pursuing meaning in a world where intelligence is abundant and necessity no longer supplies it by default.

An autodidact, husband, and father of five, Dickinson lives in the United States with his family, continuing to build learning tools that help people stay anchored as the future accelerates.

Follow: **@learningengpub** on X

Made in the USA
Monee, IL
04 November 2026

67375848R00059